HUMVEES

BY DENNY VON FINN

EPIC

BELLWETHER MEDIA · MINNEAPOLIS, MN

EPIC BOOKS are no ordinary books. They burst with intense action, high-speed heroics, and shadows of the unknown. Are you ready for an Epic adventure?

This edition first published in 2013 by Bellwether Media, Inc.

No part of this publication may be reproduced in whole or in part without written permission of the publisher. For information regarding permission, write to Bellwether Media, Inc., Attention: Permissions Department, 5357 Penn Avenue South, Minneapolis, MN 55419.

Library of Congress Cataloging-in-Publication Data

Von Finn, Denny.
  Humvees / by Denny Von Finn.
    p. cm. – (Epic: military vehicles)
  Summary: "Engaging images accompany information about Humvees. The combination of high-interest subject matter and light text is intended for students in grades 2 through 7"–Provided by publisher.
  Audience: Ages 6-12.
  Includes bibliographical references and index.
  ISBN 978-1-60014-886-6 (hbk. : alk. paper)
  1. Hummer trucks–Juvenile literature. I. Title.
  UG618.V56 2013
  623.74'722–dc23   2012036104

Printed in the United States of America, North Mankato, MN.

The photographs in this book are reproduced through the courtesy of the United States Department of Defense. A special thanks to Ted Carlson/Fotodynamics for contributing the photo on pp. 16-17 and Stephen Morton/Getty Images for the photo on pp. 8-9.

TABLE OF CONTENTS

HUMVEES

A U.S. Army Humvee speeds across the desert. Its big tires kick sand into the air. Inside, eight soldiers are ready for battle.

Enemy bullets hit the Humvee. They barely dent its **armor** and thick glass. The Humvee skids to a stop.

Latitude

Longitude

7

MACHINE GUN

GUNNER

A **gunner** on top of the Humvee fires quick bursts from the **machine gun**. The brave soldiers leap from the Humvee and into action.

ARMOR, WEAPONS, AND FEATURES

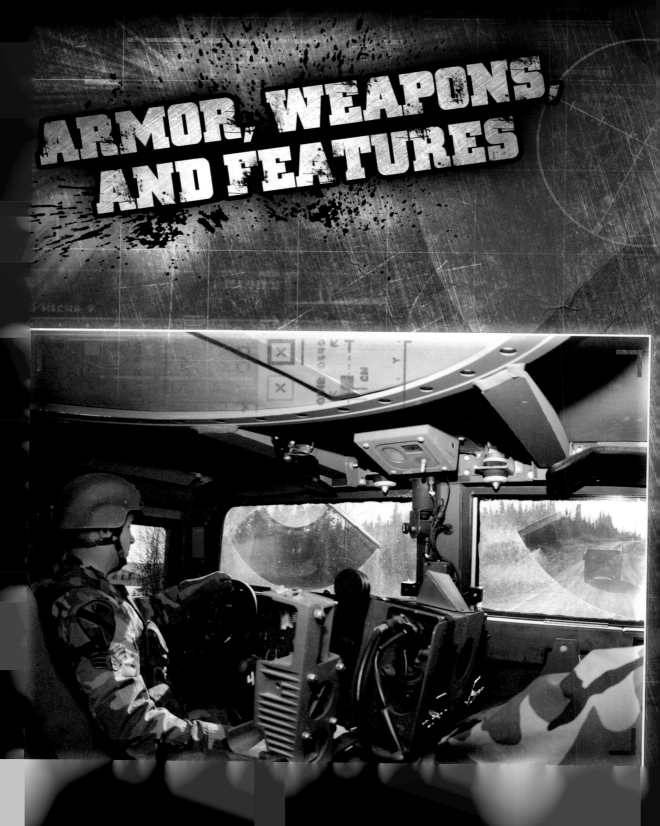

A Humvee looks like a jeep with muscles. Its thick armor protects the soldiers inside.

Humvee Fact

Humvee is short for "High-Mobility Multipurpose Wheeled Vehicle."

TURRET

MISSILE

Humvees carry powerful weapons. The gunner controls a **turret** on top of some Humvees. Other Humvees use **missiles** to take down large targets like helicopters.

A Humvee can go almost anywhere. Tall tires keep the vehicle high above the ground. **Four-wheel drive** helps it power over rough land.

Humvee Fact

Some Humvees can be fitted with tracks to help them move through deep snow.

TRACKS

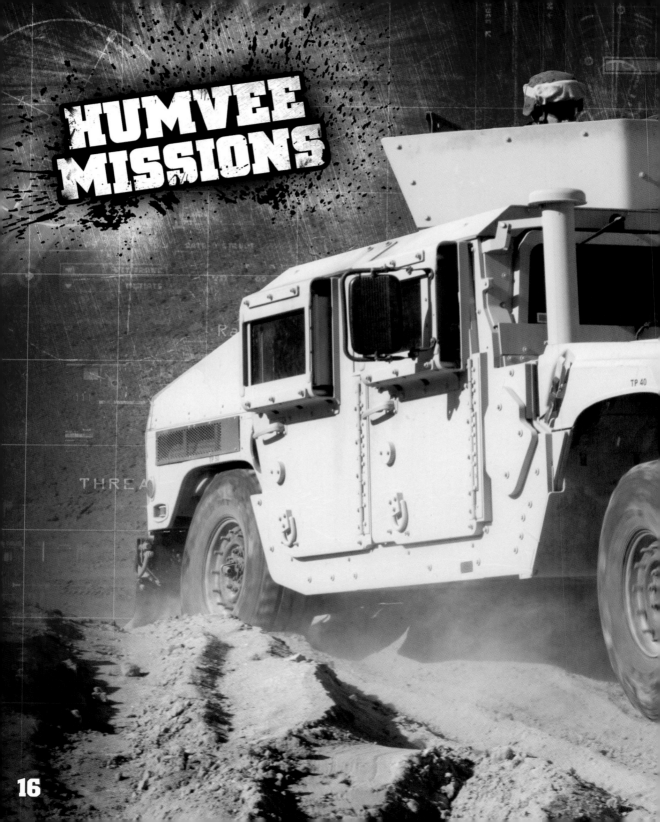

HUMVEE MISSIONS

Humvees perform many **missions**. They bring troops into dangerous areas. They also deliver **cargo** to soldiers and **civilians**.

Humvees help soldiers **scout** behind enemy lines. They are always prepared for a fight.

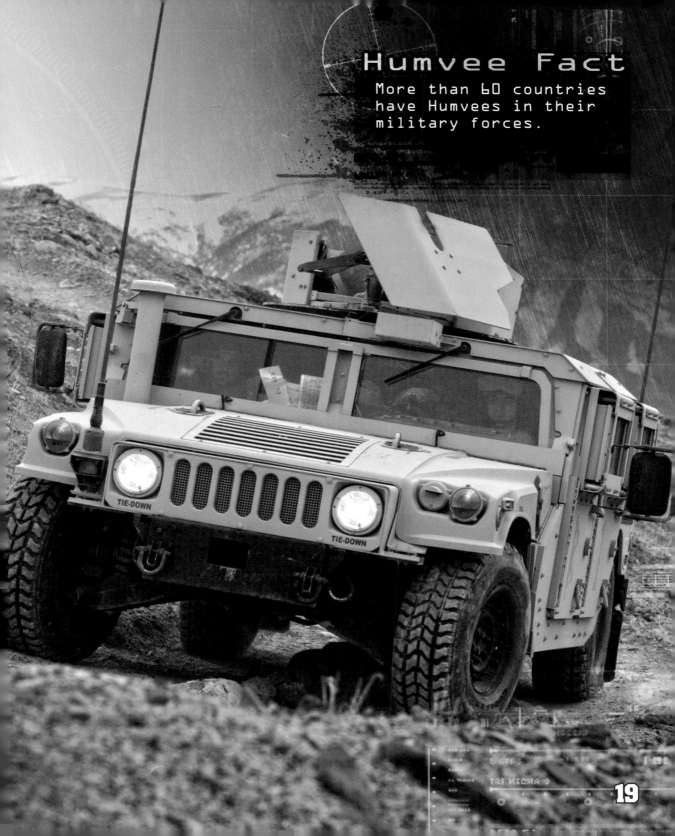

Humvee Fact

More than 60 countries
have Humvees in their
military forces.

VEHICLE BREAKDOWN: HUMVEE

Used By:	U.S. Air Force
	U.S. Army
	U.S. Marine Corps
	U.S. Navy
Entered Service:	1985
Length:	15 feet (4.6 meters)
Height:	6 feet (1.8 meters)
Width:	7.1 feet (2.2 meters)
Weight:	5,200 pounds (2,359 kilograms)
Top Speed:	around 70 miles (113 kilometers) per hour
Range:	350 miles (563 kilometers)
Crew:	2 to 4
Weapons:	machine gun, missiles
Primary Missions:	troop transport, ambulance, cargo transport

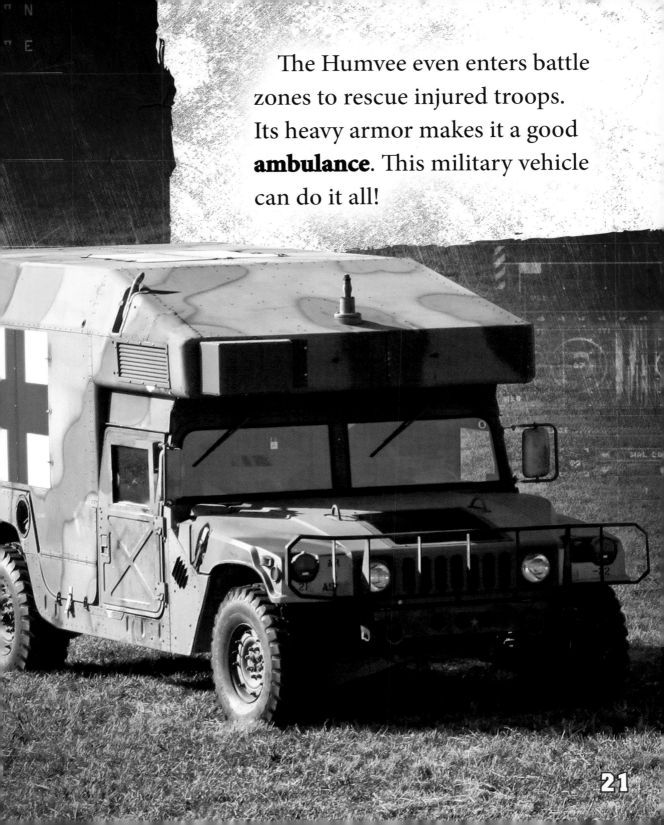

The Humvee even enters battle zones to rescue injured troops. Its heavy armor makes it a good **ambulance**. This military vehicle can do it all!

GLOSSARY

ambulance—a vehicle that brings injured people to hospitals

armor—thick steel plates that protect passengers from bullets and other weapons

cargo—supplies that are carried inside a vehicle

civilians—people who are not in the military

four-wheel drive—a feature that allows all four wheels to receive power from the engine

gunner—the crew member who operates the Humvee's machine gun

machine gun—a weapon that rapidly fires bullets

missiles—explosives that are guided to a target

missions—military tasks

scout—to search for information

turret—a platform that holds the main gun and can turn in any direction

TO LEARN MORE

At the Library

David, Jack. *Humvees*. Minneapolis, Minn.: Bellwether Media, 2009.

Hamilton, John. *Humvees*. Edina, Minn.: ABDO Pub. Co., 2012.

Kaelberer, Angie Peterson. *U.S. Army Humvees*. Mankato, Minn.: Capstone Press, 2007.

On the Web

Learning more about Humvees is as easy as 1, 2, 3.

1. Go to www.factsurfer.com.

2. Enter "Humvees" into the search box.

3. Click the "Surf" button and you will see a list of related Web sites.

With factsurfer.com, finding more information is just a click away.

INDEX